Elephants For Kids

Amazing Animal Books
for Young Readers

By Kim Chase

Mendon Cottage Books

JD-Biz Publishing

Download Free Books!
http://MendonCottageBooks.com

All Rights Reserved.
No part of this publication may be reproduced in any form or by any means, including scanning, photocopying, or otherwise without prior written permission from JD-Biz Corp and http://AmazingAnimalBooks.com. Copyright © 2015

All Images Licensed by Fotolia and 123RF

Read More Amazing Animal Books

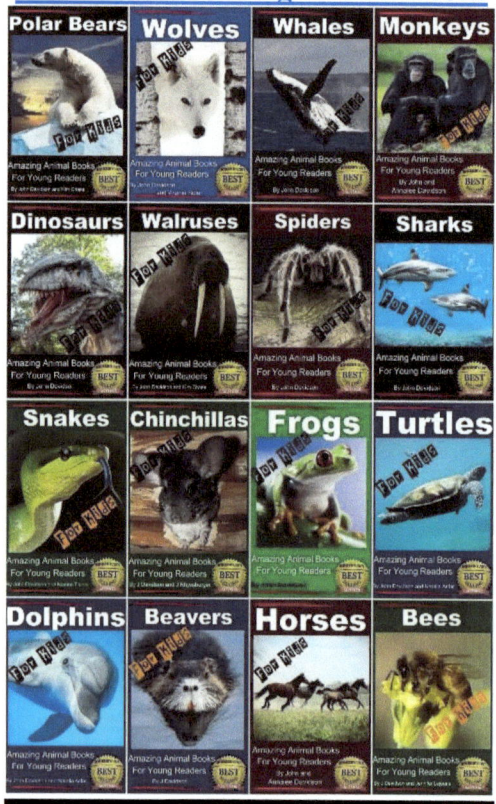

Purchase at Amazon.com

Download Free Books!
http://MendonCottageBooks.com

Table of Contents

Introduction

The world of elephants is a fascinating place! There is so much we can learn about them, and yet there are still mysteries about them waiting to be revealed. There may be stories you have heard about elephants. Now the question is, "Are those stores fact or fiction? Are they true or false?"

One bit of information you may have heard is that elephants have a good memory. That is very true! It is so true, that it is believed that elephants have a better memory than humans do. Elephants can remember other elephants that they may not have seen in years. They can also remember being treated unkindly by someone even though many years may have passed.

Another story that is often thought about with elephants is, "Are they afraid of mice?" You might have heard that elephants fear mice because they can run up the elephant's trunk. But the answer here is that this story is not true, and there is no proof of any kind to support this.

It may not surprise you know that the elephants of today are related to the Ice Age Mammoth. At one time there were over 350 different species of elephants, yet today we
have only two species left! Can you name the two species? What you may be surprised to learn is that elephants were not always the large creatures you see today. In fact, in prehistoric times, the elephant was as small as the size of a cow or pig. Would it surprise you to learn that the elephants of today are related to the sea cow known as the Manatee?

Did you know that when the elephants flap their ears they do it for a reason? Or do you know what jobs the elephants use their tusks for? An elephant's tusk can be smaller on one side than the other. Do you know the reason why? Did you know that a female elephant will spend her whole life in one herd, while the male elephant usually live their lives alone sometime after the age of 14?

As you can see, there are many interesting things that can be learned about this tremendous sized animal with the ivory tusks.

About Elephants

It is believed that long ago there were greater than 350 elephant species that roamed the earth. Now we have two species left in the world. Those remaining species are the African and the Asian elephants. Each one of those species has a sub species.

The sub-species that would fall under the Asian group are the Sumatran, Indian, Sri Lanka, and the Borneo. (The Borneo elephants are also known as the Pygmy). Exciting news is that right now, researchers are exploring the possibility that there may be a fifth sub species to add to this group, but it is still too early to tell for sure since testing is still being done. The Elephants that are a part of this group; can be recognized by their big bodies; but they have smaller ears than the African elephants, and only the males have tusks.

What is interesting about the African sub-species is that they are named after the locations they live in. In this group, the sub-species are the Savannah, and the Forest elephants. The Savannah elephants are also known as the Bush elephants. These elephants are the largest worldwide. In this species, both the female and the males have tusks.

There has been a great deal of research done on the African and Asian elephants. What is known at this point is that elephants are very smart and affectionate animals. These animals seem to adapt well to changes.

Here is something interesting to consider. When you stop and think about elephants, the first image that probably comes to mind is an enormous sized animal. Would you be surprised to find out that during prehistoric times there were some species of elephants that were small sized? Yes, it is true! DNA tests prove that some species were the size of cows and pigs. Another startling fact is that there is some relationship between elephants and the current day sea cows known as Manatees.

Yet another interesting fact about elephants is their ability to learn. Research has been conducted through games as well as other materials to prove this fact. It has also been discovered that they are capable of learning a great deal of information. Their memories are considered to be the best worldwide, and their memories are even greater than humans!

The Evolution of Elephants

It is believed that elephants can be traced back to approximately 2,000 B.C. Because of their large size, they were selected to help with any building that was done during that time. Although the Mammoth is extinct, experts do feel that the Mammoth was an early representative of elephants. Experts further feel that the elephants we see today are the descendants of the Mammoth. You may wonder how that is possible especially since the elephants of today look so different from their ancestor the Mammoth. This can be explained through the process of evolution.

Many changes in the elephant's appearance started to occur. One of the first changes that you may immediately notice is the loss of their thick looking coat. In the Ice Age, Mammoths roamed the earth. It was necessary for them to have this warm hair to protect them from the temperatures during that time. But when the Ice Age came to a close, and the temperatures started to rise, the elephants no longer had a need for their warm coat. So their warm thick coats was replaced by thicker skins and larger sized ears. They used their ears as fans to help cool them down when they got hot.

Yet another change that took place was with their trunk. The elephants' ancestors had trunks, but they weren't as long and they didn't rely on them as much as the elephants of today. The elephants of today use their trunks for many things, but one of their trunks main functions is to give them the ability to grasp at objects. Yet another change was with their tusks. Experts believe that their early ancestors actually had a set of two tusks. One set of tusks was on their upper jaw, and the second set of tusks was attached to their lower jaw. The elephants of today have one set of tusks.

The evolution process was a slow process. Not every species of elephant was able to adapt to their ever-changing environment. That explains why they are not with us today. Elephants are amazing animals and their story of evolution is a successful one. Their evolution process began approximately 50 – 60 million years back, and it because of their fight to survive, and their ability to adapt, that these wonderful creatures are with us today.

Elephant Features

When you think about the features of an elephant do you think of their amazing trunks, beautiful ivory tusks, their large flapping ears, or just their immense size? As you may already know, elephants are the largest land animals in the world today. Each part of their anatomy is helpful to the elephant to survive in their environment. But it is the elephant's trunk that is the most important to them.

Because their trunk has over 40,000 muscles, it allows the elephant to move their trunk in many different positions, and gives them the ability to grasp and to pick up objects. Their trunks are also very strong. In fact, they could uproot large trees from the ground if they needed to. The elephants also use their trunks to communicate with, and for their sense of smell.

Even though an elephant has a total of about 24 sharp teeth, they only put to use two or three of these teeth at one time. Since the elephants are plant eaters, they first use their teeth to tear up the different plants they eat, and then they use their teeth again to chew up their food. Because they use only a few of their teeth at a time, their teeth do not get a chance to wear down evenly. Their teeth are grown from the backs of their jaws then their teeth go forward and replace any missing teeth.

Tusks are considered to be a part of the elephant's teeth. These tusks will keep on growing even after an elephant has completely matured. An elephant's age can be determined by how long their tusks are. These tusks can be also be used as tools. Sometimes elephants dig with their tusks to search for water. Other times, elephants use their tusk for removing tree bark. This is done so that they can eat the pulp that can be found underneath. In the African species of elephant, both the male and female have tusks. However, the male tusks usually grow longer. It is not uncommon for one of the tusks to be shorter than the other. This is caused because the elephant uses one side more than the other. An elephant's tusks are made of beautiful ivory. This ivory is very valuable and highly sought after by people. It is one reason why elephants are killed.

But laws have been put into place to make that practice illegal.

An elephant's skin is about 1" thick and is covered with small hairs. Even though they have thick skin, their skin is still very sensitive to sunlight. To help protect themselves from the sun's rays, an elephant will try to cover their skin with dirt or mud. To help the elephant control their body temperature and keep cool, they flap their large sized ears, and use them just like a fan.

An elephant can get a good deal of traction from their huge legs. But an elephant is not able to run, and they do not move quickly. What they do instead is walk at a steady speed for hours and hours.

Where Elephants Live

Because of the many food choices elephant eat, they can be found in very different settings. For example, elephants can be found living in grassland areas or in the Savannah desert. Then again, they can be found in forests where swamps are present. The only wild elephants currently live in Africa and Asia. They live in subtropical and tropical regions.

The elephants live in regions that have different amounts of daylight hours. However, because of their poor eyesight that tends to worsen at nighttime, and the amount of hours it takes them each day to gather enough food to eat, they prefer a region that can give them about 12

hours per day of daylight. The more hours they have of daylight, the easier it will be for them to get enough food to eat, or search for their needed water.

Year after year, elephants follow migrational paths that they make during their journey, getting from one place to another. These paths are clear evidence that elephants have roamed in that area. These paths also allow the elephants to enjoy the plant vegetation that grows in the different areas that they roam.

Elephants can travel between 12 – 21 miles each day. But the amount of miles traveled can depend on how old the elephants are in the herd and what the land terrain is like. They are aided in their travels by having a great instinct for direction, and their endurance for traveling for long periods of time without getting tired.

Elephants can eat over 50 tons of plant vegetation each day. One problem occurs when an elephant is confined to certain areas and not allowed to roam freely. The elephants can totally eat the vegetation that is grown there, and it is hard for these plants to then re-grow. On the other hand, when the elephants are not confined and are welcomed to freely roam, there are environmental benefits. They clear plants and trees away so new vegetation can grow in its place.

For many elephants in Africa, they can be found living in National Parks. These parks were set up to help protect the elephants and to try to give them enough room to help their population thrive. Elephants have a natural instinct to roam, and to know when it is time for them to move on. Because they can adjust and adapt to their new habitat surroundings, the elephants are able to survive.

Elephants may also live in captivity. Zoos try hard to make certain that they have enough food and water and activities for the elephants so that they do not get bored. But for some elephants in captivity that do not have ample room to roam, they can find it very stressful since their natural way of life and their instinct is for them to roam freely and at their own speed.

How Elephants Eat

Elephants are fascinating to watch when they eat. Elephants are very smart animals, and they put their brain skills to good use in their hunt for food. Their size and strength give them a clear advantage over other animals. From the ground, elephants can reach higher than other animals. If they can't reach their intended food source (such as fruits) with their trunks, then they can simply wrap their trunk around the tree and try to shake the fruits loose. This will bring down some food for their group and young ones to eat. If shaking the tree doesn't get the fruit down, then the elephants can take their mighty trunk and pull the plant or tree right out from the ground, and then eat it. Elephants eat many types of food including fruits and plants. They eat leaves, twigs, tree roots, grass and other vegetation that may be growing in the area they are in.

One huge problem that elephants face today is that their habitat is constantly getting smaller in the wild. This creates a problem of lack of food. This decrease of food sources can make the elephants compete with one another for whatever food is available.

Even though elephants can search for food for more than 16 hours each day, they only digest 40% of what they eat. Experts are still trying to understand why more of their food doesn't get digested. Elephants take in water through their trunks. Since elephants can drink nearly 15 quarts (14 liters) of water at once, it can be difficult for them to find enough water during certain times of the year. It is during this dry season, that the elephants will use their trunks to dig holes in the ground in search of water that may be hiding below the surface. If the elephants are successful in their search for water, then once they leave the area, other wild animals will come and also use this water.

It is felt by some people that elephants can damage the environment because of their eating habits. But if an elephant is able to roam freely, then they can actually help the environment. Elephants will move along before they consume all of the vegetation in one area. As the elephants eat the existing plant life, it actually clears the area for more vegetation to grow. It can be a problem if an elephant becomes confined in an area is not given the chance to roam freely. That is when the chances are high that the elephants will eat all the vegetation that they see.

How Elephants Communicate

Elephants can speak to each other using both verbal as well as non-verbal means. When elephants choose to communicate verbally, they often express themselves through loud trumpeting. So what does this trumpeting mean? The trumpeting is done at different levels depending on whom the elephant is trying to reach. This trumpeting sound can be heard for miles and could be a warning sign of danger, aggression or even excitement.

A young elephant is called a calf. These calves learn the sounds of their mother's call from an early age. The mother will send out different sounds to her calf. Sometimes the mother will send out trumpeting noises to scold or encourage her calf, as well as making sure that their calves keep up with the herd. But not all of the verbal sounds an elephant makes are loud. Elephants can also send out low sounds like a growl or a grunt when they communicate.

So how do they communicate using non-verbal means? This is usually done by contact. One sign of affection or excitement is wrapping their trunk around one another. Or when they rub their bodies together. You may consider this similar to a human handshake or a hug.

It has been observed that mother elephants are very affectionate to their young ones. There are demonstrations of touching the calves with their mother's trunks. This may be the equal to human mothers when they pat their children on their heads. Another non-verbal communication is the trunk position of the elephant. If their trunks are down, then it can be taken to be that the elephant is friendly. However if their trunks are raised, it could be a sign that a male is behaving a bit aggressively and standing firm. When there is another elephant male with their trunk also raised then this could be thought of as a threat.

It has been discussed that elephants are very intelligent, and seem to show many emotions that are close to those emotions experienced by humans. Elephants have shown the emotion of comfort for each other, as well as having the ability to be sad and to cry.

Experts have done a wonderful job in trying to understand the communication level between elephants, but some mysteries still exist. One part of their communication skill that they are still trying to unravel is when danger is near. There is one elephant in the herd that will send out a trumpet warning. The question becomes which elephant should send out the warning to the other members in their herd? It is not known how this is decided. It has been noted that it is not always the elephant in charge, and that it is not always the same elephant that sends out the warning each time. As you can see, there are still many mysteries that surround these amazing animals.

Life In The Herd

Life in an elephant heard is very interesting. The female elephant will spend her whole life within one herd. But the male elephant will leave the herd at about the age of 14. Female elephants are very social to one another. She will interact not only with those within her own herd, but will interact with other herds as well.

There are times when one herd will split and a smaller herd will be formed. Even if a second herd is formed, the elephants have a long memory and can actually remember anyone that was a part of the original herd. They will go on being friendly to each other if they meet up again.

Male elephants lead a more isolated life. Once they start growing older, their position within the herd changes. They move from traveling from the middle of the herd, to the outer edges. Young elephants are usually found traveling in the middle of the herd. As the males get older, they start to venture out on their own. At first they leave the herd for only a few days. But each time they venture out on their own, they start to increase the amount of time they are away from the herd, until one day they just don't return to their herd at all.

At this point, the males may come together and form a bachelor herd, but many males leave this type of herd because of the tension. There is always a great deal of aggression, as the males fight to see who will be in charge of the herd. This challenging of each other will happen often. A weak male could also be forced to leave the herd.

Elephants enjoy playing, and they can be seen playing in the herd. When they have enough food and water there is time for them to be carefree and play. Other times, if their food becomes scarce, or there is danger that is close by, then the mood of the herd will change to being serious and protective.

Elephants are very smart. It has been determined that in a mirror they can identify themselves. These elephants also know themselves not only as individuals, but they are also aware of their place in the herd.

African Elephants

Of the two species of Elephants left in the world today – the Asian and the African elephants – the African is the largest. Their ears are very big, and both the females and males grow tusks. The male tusks grow to a larger size than those of the females.

These animals stand over 12 ft. tall (3.6 meters) and can weight more than 14,000 lbs. (6350 kg). Some of the sub species of the

African elephant are much smaller in height and weight. The members of the sub species group weigh approximately 7500 lbs. (3401 kg) and stand nearly 9 ft. tall (2.7 meters).

In the desert of the Savannah is the place where you will find many of these elephants. The thick forest areas are another place where they make themselves at home. The size of their herd numbers between 12 – 20 elephants.

Asian Elephants

Asian elephants hold a special place in Asian culture. The elephant is looked upon with respect and as symbols of wisdom, intelligence and strength. It is because of their sheer strength that elephants have replaced machinery in moving heavy logs from their forests. In return for their hard work, the elephants are treated very well. Asian elephants seem less aggressive to people than African elephants.

Asian elephants have huge bodies, but their ears are small than those of the African species. In this group, only the male elephant will grow tusks. Full-grown Asian male elephants stand about 12 feet tall (3.6 meters), and can weigh nearly 11,000 lbs. (4989 kg).

Young Asian elephants enjoying a swim

Asian elephants can be found in India, Sri Lanka as well as Bangladesh. Because their natural habitat keeps changing, these elephants can also be found in Nepal, Indonesia, as well as Indochina.

Fun Elephant Facts

Let's conclude with some interesting elephant facts that you may not have known before. For instance, did you know that...

Elephants are considered to be the largest land animal worldwide! Their tusks can grow to an impressive length of 10 ft., and weigh nearly 200 lbs. It is thought that the elephant relies on one tusk more than the other. This tusk that they use more often is referred to as their dominant tusk. Because they use one of their tusks more often, it explains why one of the elephant's tusks is usually shorter. It is just like people being left or right handed, and they tend to use that hand more often. An elephant's trunk has over 40,000 muscles!

26,000 lbs. (11793 kg) is the weight of the heaviest elephant ever recorded. An elephant's brain is the biggest as compared to other animals worldwide, and weighs in at 11 lbs. (4.9 kg). A newly born elephant can weigh as much as 260 lbs. (117 kg). Although these newborns are able to stand up soon after their birth, they are born blind, and will need the help of their mothers and their trunks to help and guide them.

Elephants have both excellent hearing as well as a sense of smell, but their eyesight is poor. If you were wondering, it is simply not true that elephants have a fear for mice. Elephants are not able to run. In the wild, an elephant can live between 50 – 70 years, and 82 was the recorded age of the oldest elephant ever known to exist. The word "elephant" can be traced back to ancient times, and the meaning of the word is ivory.

Elephants enjoy swimming, and also drink a great deal of water. In fact, an elephant can drink almost 15 quarts (14 liters) at one time. Their diet consists of eating an assortment of plants. They forage for food nearly 16 hrs. each day, and can eat between 300 – 600 lbs. (136 – 272 kg.) of food per day!

Many times when you see elephants in a circus, at a zoo, or hard at work, these are usually female elephants. The females are chosen for those jobs, as they appear to be more agreeable than the male elephants. The males can go through periods when they become very aggressive.

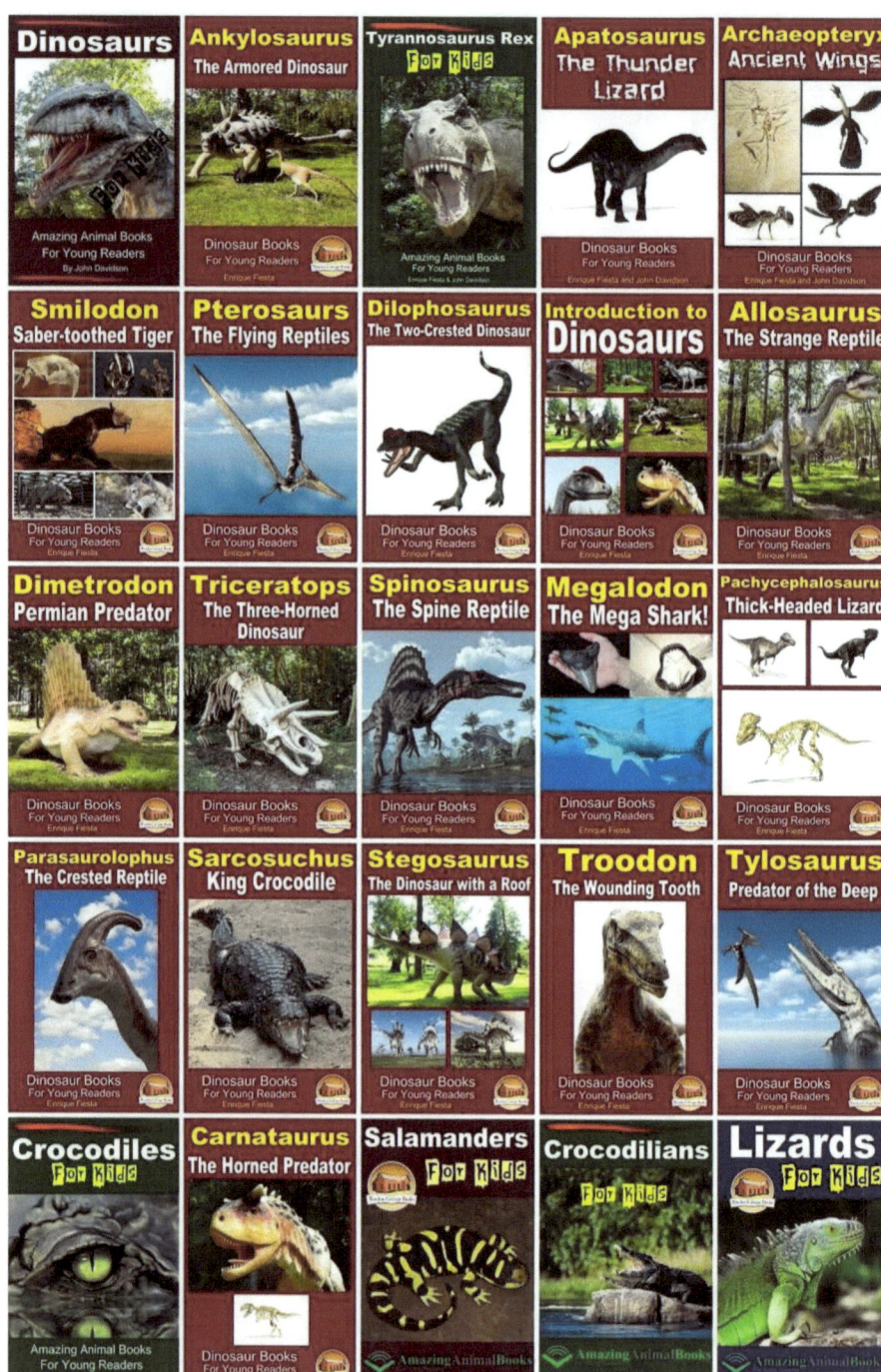

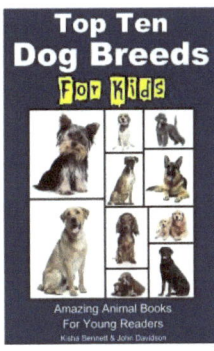

Top Ten Dog Breeds For Kids

Amazing Animal Books For Young Readers
Kisha Bennett & John Davidson

German Shepherds

Dog Books for Kids
K. Bennett

Bulldogs

Dog Books for Kids
K. Bennett

Dachshund

Dog Books for Kids
K. Bennett

Poodles

Dog Books for Kids
K. Bennett

Labrador Retrievers

Dog Books for Kids
K. Bennett

Rottweilers

Dog Books for Kids
K. Bennett

Boxers

Dog Books for Kids
K. Bennett

Golden Retrievers

Dog Books for Kids
K. Bennett

Puppies
Dog Books For Kids

Amazing Animal Books
By John Davidson

Beagles

Dog Books for Kids
K. Bennett

Yorkshire Terriers

Dog Books for Kids
K. Bennett

Dogs
Top Ten Dog Breeds For Kids

Amazing Animal Books For Young Readers
Zahra Jazeel & John Davidson

Cats For Kids

Amazing Animal Books For Young Readers
K. Bennett & John Davidson

Foxes For Kids

Amazing Animal Books For Young Readers
Zahra Jazeel & John Davidson

Wolves For Kids

Amazing Animal Books For Young Readers
By John Davidson and Virginia Fidler

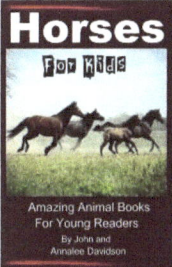

Horses
For Kids
Amazing Animal Books
For Young Readers
By John and Annalee Davidson

Wolves
For Kids
Amazing Animal Books
For Young Readers
By John Davidson and Virginia Fidler

Lady Bugs
For Kids
Amazing Animal Books
For Young Readers
By Jean Hall & John Davidson

Sasquatch - Yeti Abominable Snowman Bigfoot
For Kids
Amazing Animal Books
For Young Readers
By John Davidson

Penguins
For Kids
Amazing Animal Books
For Young Readers
Kim Chase & John Davidson

Komodo Dragons
For Kids
Amazing Animal Books
For Young Readers
By Lisa Barry & John Davidson

Cats
For Kids
Amazing Animal Books
For Young Readers
K. Bennett & John Davidson

Spiders
For Kids
Amazing Animal Books
For Young Readers
By John Davidson

Giant Panda Bears
For Kids
Amazing Animal Books
For Young Readers
By John Davidson

Animals of North America
For Kids
Amazing Animal Books
For Young Readers
By John Davidson

Birds of North America
For Kids
Amazing Animal Books
For Young Readers
By John Davidson

Dolphins
For Kids
Amazing Animal Books
For Young Readers
By John Davidson and Natalia Asfar

Hamsters
For Kids
Amazing Animal Books
For Young Readers
John Davidson

Polar Bears
For Kids
Amazing Animal Books
For Young Readers
By John Davidson and Kim Chase

Turtles
For Kids
Amazing Animal Books
For Young Readers
By John Davidson and Natalia Asfar

Walruses
For Kids
Amazing Animal Books
For Young Readers
By John Davidson and Kim Chase

My First Book About Animals of Australia
Amazing Animal Books
By Annalee and John Davidson
Children's Picture Books

Goats
For Kids
Amazing Animal Books
For Young Readers
Rachel Smith & John Davidson

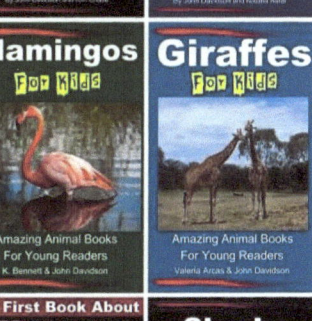

Flamingos
For Kids
Amazing Animal Books
For Young Readers
K. Bennett & John Davidson

Giraffes
For Kids
Amazing Animal Books
For Young Readers
Valeria Arcas & John Davidson

Eagles
For Kids
Amazing Animal Books
For Young Readers
Nicholas Williams & John Davidson

Bears
For Kids
Amazing Animal Books
For Young Readers
Zahra Jazeel & John Davidson

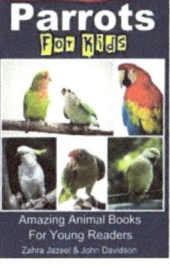

Parrots
For Kids
Amazing Animal Books
For Young Readers
Zahra Jazeel & John Davidson

My First Book About Kittens
Amazing Animal Books
By John Davidson
Children's Picture Books

Sharks
For Kids
Amazing Animal Books
For Young Readers
By John Davidson

Our books are available at

1. Amazon.com
2. Barnes and Noble
3. Itunes
4. Kobo
5. Smashwords
6. Google Play Books

Download Free Books!
http://MendonCottageBooks.com

Publisher

JD-Biz Corp

P O Box 374

Mendon, Utah 84325

http://www.jd-biz.com/

Mendon Cottage Books

P O Box 374, Mendon Utah 84325

www.ingramcontent.com/pod-product-compliance
Lightning Source LLC
Chambersburg PA
CBHW050848290526
45792CB00002B/563